BODY OF MUSIC

By Stacey Culpepper
Illustrations by Stephanie Para

ISBN-13: 978-0996138420

Library of Congress Control Number
2015911077
Diverse Culpepper Books- Rialto, CA

What does a girl do to overcome her stage fright? This story is written for girls and boys of all ages. Melody will encourage young readers to work hard to overcome any obstacle that stand in the way of positive goals they set out to achieve.

This book is dedicated to my husband Charles, Mom, Dad, April, Robee, and Maurice.

Stacey Culpepper has been writing since the age of seven. She decided to make her works public because she saw a great need for diversity in YA literature and storytellers. Living in diverse environments stimulated her already active imagination at a young age and enhanced her zest for multiculturalism. Stacey believes young readers need to see themselves in positive writings in order to thrive. Her goal is to make diverse stories easily accessible to young people everywhere.

Stephanie Para has a background in painting, photography, and writing. She attended California State University of San Bernardino. She is actively involved in community service work and uses her art and photography skills to help others. She draws inspiration from her faith, family, and friends, to create imaginative and unique illustrations. Stephanie lives in California with her mother and feline Kitty.

BODY OF MUSIC

Melody had the most soothing voice when she sang. She knew she wanted to be a singer since she was five years old. But, she would always get butterflies and freeze up when she had to sing in front of other people. She looked at her long, curly, light-brown hair in the floor length mirror in her room, "la, la, llooovvvee", Melody began to sing and just then her mom walked in,

"Oh mom!" Melody squeaked instead of singing.

"Well sweetheart, how are you going to perform for nani and papa's anniversary next Saturday if you can't sing in front of me?" her mom shrugged.

"That is why I am trying to practice right now mom. I have to imagine my voice and the musical notes drifting in the air, and then I can relax." Melody sighed.

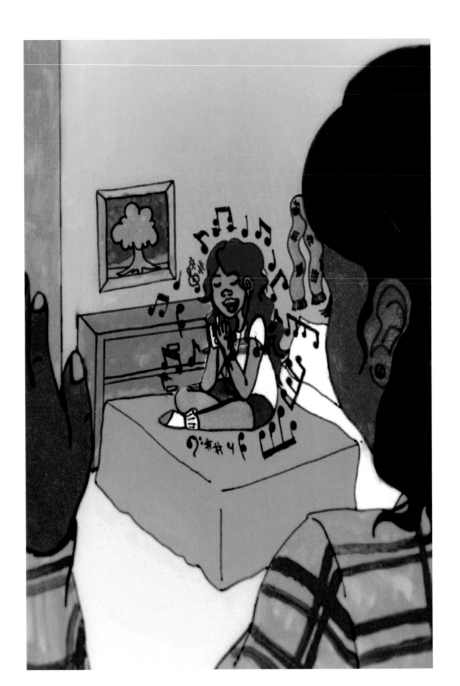

Her mom made a funny face and closed the door. But, Melody knew she had to get over her nervousness because she loved music and loved to sing. As far as she could remember music was always floating around her. Her mother was a background R&B singer and played the piano. Her dad was a trumpet player for the local salsa band 'Brooklyn Heights'. Her paternal grandparents traveled through Puerto Rico as a singing duo with the band 'Las Sonrisas' before Melody's dad was born. There was always a radio, cd, or musicians playing in her house.

Melody loved Saturday mornings because she would go to band practice with her dad. Before they would leave she would watch her dad take his trumpet apart and carefully clean all the pieces. He would shine the trumpet until the gold glistened from the sunlight that hit it from the kitchen window. Melody would hum the entire time and when she saw her dad put the trumpet together again, she knew it was time to pack up and go to rehearsal.

After a short walk to the subway and a ride on the A train for about ten minutes, they walked four blocks to the jazz club. It was so bright and noisy in the city, but when they walked inside, their eyes could not adjust before their ears could hear Hector's saxophone drifting inside the club. "Hey Melody" all the guys shouted as the door closed and made the club dark.

"Hi Hector, Chelito and Buns" Melody said blinking her eyes quickly so she could see much clearly.

Melody saw the stage and the next thing she remembered was hearing the beautiful tunes the instruments were playing. Melody watched Chelito slide the arm of his trombone, and Buns began to tap out a soft beat on his drums. She chuckled when Hector poked out his lips as he started to play the bass. Her dad's trumpet glowed under the lights.

She loved how all the instruments sounded when the guys played together. She would close her eyes and twirl between tables singing to herself. She imagined the musical notes wrapped around her body giving her the feeling of a nice warm hug.

"Come on up baby girl," her dad said as he held out his hand to pull her up on stage.

All of a sudden Melody felt the darkness of the club encircle her. She thought they all could see her knees knocking as she walked up the steps.

"Papi, I have to save my voice for the party next Saturday," Melody said trembling. The truth was she could not even sing in front of her dad's band mates, and she had known them since she was three years old.

"Everyone does a rehearsal before the event Melody," her father said brushing a stray curl from her face.

"I have practiced every day before and after school, I know I will be ready next Saturday," she said with tears filling her eyes.

The guys looked at each other nervously. They watched Melody shuffle off stage towards the back of the club.

"Okay guys, let's take it from the top!" her dad counted, "uno, dos, uno, dos, tres, cuatro."

That whole week Melody got up an hour early to practice her song. Her parents were worried her voice would be hoarse by Saturday so her mom made her drink two glasses of water every morning at breakfast. She had to ask her homeroom teacher for a bathroom pass every day.

The sound of her dad's trumpet whispered to Melody in her sleep. She heard him playing her papa's favorite chorus and then she realized that song was not in her dreams. Melody jumped out of bed and headed straight towards the shower. She knew it was Saturday. Once she was dressed, her dad was waiting at the bottom stairs for her to come down.

"Hey pretty girl, are you ready to make some music today?" her father said smiling with his teeth whiter than the keys of a piano.

Her dad always smelled like fresh soap and his smile was so bright, it could light up an entire room.

"Ahhh! Yes papi," Melody said yawning.

"So, how do you feel about performing for nani and papa's anniversary?"

"I feel a little jittery, but I know I'm not going to freeze up on stage tonight." But, just as she said it, Melody felt butterflies in her stomach.

Her father put down his trumpet mouth piece and gave her a tight bear hug.

"That's my girl!" her dad flashed a smile.

Later that afternoon the entire family took the A train to the club. It was always fun to be really dressed up on the subway because everyone would stop and stare. Papa was not happy because he hated public transportation and would mumble under his breath the whole ride. But, he was all smiles when his friends greeted him at the platform as they got off the train.

"Felicidades!" they all sang in unison, hugging and patting him on the back.

Nani rolled her eyes and sucked her teeth as she brushed past the guys. But, she had the biggest smile when she walked up the stairs and saw her friends waiting outside the club.

"Mira, mis amigas!" nani shouted in her high pitched voice.

"Felicidades Maria!" they all harmonized as they kissed and hugged nani.

The club was packed with family and friends. It was amusing to watch everyone laughing, drinking, and eating. But, the crackle of conversation didn't last long, as everyone's eyes adjusted to the stage that had just lit up.

"Now for the main part of our celebration today," Melody's father announced. "A very special performance for my lovely parents from their beautiful granddaughter, Melody!" he grinned as he adjusted the microphone to her height.

The roar of the crowd sounded just like being at a Yankee's baseball game. The whistles and cheers did not help Melody with her nerves. She got up on stage, closed her eyes, and heard her dad count, "A one, two, one, two, three, four…"

The harmonious music of the instruments began to melt together, but when Melody opened her mouth a squeaking sound came out. All she could imagine was nani, papa, and all her family staring at her. She couldn't see anything but their eyes and she felt terrified. The butterflies returned back to her stomach and she fought the urge to run off stage. She was so mad at herself for freezing up again, she blinked fast so she would not cry.

The band stopped playing one instrument by one, and Melody could see the audience anxiously shift in their seats.

"Just close your eyes and let the musical notes lift you up and let your voice fly away," Melody said to herself under her breath. She took a deep breath in and a long slow breath out.

She turned to her father and smiled confidently in the microphone, "Okay guys, let's take it from the top again!"

The entire club erupted in whistles and cheers. Melody didn't hear any of them.

She imagined the musical notes of the bass guitar, trumpet, drums and trombone floating through the beautiful clear blue sky outside and felt all the nerves leave her body. Then she heard her dad's trumpet playing the chorus to her grandparents' favorite song. Melody allowed her voice to drift gently with the music around her and belted out the most beautiful note. As she started to sing the first verse, all of the guys in the band looked at each other and smiled big. But deep inside, Melody's smile was bigger.

Please read more about Stacey and her other diverse children's book on her website @www.staceyculpepper.com

Diverse Culpepper Books

ISBN-13: 978-0996138420

ISBN-10: 0996138420

Made in the USA
San Bernardino, CA
08 September 2015